The Rose

&

The Sun

By Vinod C V

and Samantha Funnell

ISBN: 978-1-3999-8179-8

DEDICATION

I would like to dedicate this book to two beautiful Roses in my life, my daughter Gemma and mum Sally, both of whom have filled my heart with so much sunlight (Samantha)

Table of Contents

Chapter 2 -The Rose Garden

Chapter 3 - Rose Care

Chapter 4 - Tales of a Rose

Chapter 5 - Seasons and Cycles

Introduction

The Rose and the Sun

I met Vinod in 2021 being drawn to and inspired by his beautiful poetry. He is Hindu and introduced me to the teachings of Advaita Vedanta which is that God is everything and we all contain God's or our soul's essence of love deep within our hearts. This is a collaboration of both our poetry. We see the Rose as a symbol of the heart. As our heart opens fully, we realise we contain pure sunlight and our essence of love flows. This book is a story of the return to the soul. As she blossoms and allows her essence to flow freely, she embodies her true nature which is love and the nature of the soul. She realises that anything that isn't love is her thorns which are protecting her and keeping her safe in her garden but she watches them so they don't grow so big that they stop her petals from opening. She shares her love with other flowers because she knows that by receiving love, they will feel inspired to open their own petals. This is a book of love; it is the essence that unites every living being and it is our hope that in sharing our poetry and our essence of love we can inspire others into opening their own petals of the heart.

CHAPTER 1

VARIETIES OF ROSES

The Rose with Many Heads

The Rose full of flowers, so many but one
Within the Rose garden all fed by the Sun
They each raise their heads as they feed from above
The source of their happiness; purest of love
Each Rose has a fragrance unique to their own
Such beauty in all as together they grow
All aspects of love filled with light of the Sun
Their scent fills the garden, a fragrance as one

The Perfect Garden

The blessed garden of the Rose
A space where all creation grows
Her garden where she found the Sun
Is where all poetry is sung

The purest love within the Rose
May thaw the hearts in time that froze
Without the love that we all seek
The garden may seem cold and bleak

The Rose when cold, so warm indoors
The Sun within her heart, she saw
All winter's frosts move into spring
A time of hope, new life begins

The Rose, her sight, with golden tint
The veil she lifts, her petals glint
For even when the hearts are thawed
Within her garden are many flaws

But this is how her seeds will grow
When watered by the love that flows
And so she sighs and blows a kiss
Her garden perfect as it is

The Rainbow Rose

Roses are red
Many other shades too
In our garden, a rainbow
With little to do

Roses are red
With many shades too
In the rainbow of our garden
Which colour are you?

Roses are red
Oh, so many shades
In our garden of many
Of which are you made?

We are one in our garden
Our petals a hue
So many shades but
You are me and I am you

The Thorny Rose

The Rose, she has petals, she also has thorns
Each live with the other but both she adorns
All has a purpose, so neither she minds
It's part of the garden she lives in, she finds
Her thorns give her safety, protection at night
Whilst petals at dawn will fill her with light
On neither she's focused, in this she will win
And so she lifts higher to where love begins

The Climbing Rose

Tangled and weaving if left without care
Turning so wild with nobody there
Putting up walls of thorns if neglected
Deserving of love and to be so respected
When nurtured her blooms will come out one by one
Climbing so high and touching the Sun
Breathe in her scent and send her your love
Her roots become stronger as she stretches above
Give her some care and honour the Rose
She will pass on her fragrance that she alone knows

The Mystical Rose

The path of a mystic
A solitary way
A pavement for one
With love guiding each day

A mystical Rose
Found deeply inside
Within a vast mansion
Her lover resides

In seven soul chambers
Her journey she travelled
Each doorway she passed through
Love's mysteries unravelled

We're each on a journey
Some mystical minds
Whichever your pathway
Just let it unwind

The Pink Rose

As you are dreaming tonight in your sleep
I wrap you in petals of crimson so deep
To keep you in gentleness, healing you'll feel
The warmth of the Rose is a feeling so real
In healing your heart, she will gently assist
Releasing your feelings, which always persist
The softness of pink surrounding you now
You'll sleep like a baby and never know how

The White Rose

The garden of white in its presence of peace
Alone in the silence, the stillness, release
The purest of Rose as she climbs from her bed
Surrounded by daisies of many a head
Sweet hollyhocks flock in her presence, to feel
The butterflies cabbage, so swift; full of zeal
Whilst all this fluttering, flitting and flows
They all feel the peace of the whitest of Rose

The Black Rose

She lies in harmony with the light
Enfolded in a blanket of divine bliss
The feminine, the dark, the womb, the moon bringing balance
The shadow reflecting the light of the Sun
Illuminating her beauty

So soft and sensual, evocative
Whispering secrets into the ears of those who will listen
Full of magic, desire and wildness
She howls with the moon and screams through the trees

Untamed and untameable, sending the hearts of men wild with desire
A warrior, fierce to those who threaten her kin
Enfolding those around her in her soft petals

A dream watcher clasping you in her velvet cloak
She has the strongest thorns but the most delicate scent
Standing alone as she is feared
Seeing her darkness, they run and hide

Only those with eyes to truly see her beauty
The Black Rose, solitary in her rose bed
Without her….
There would be no garden

Rose Buds

The tiniest bud, the youngest of flower
The innocent love in a blossom, we shower
So young and so fresh, full of joy and delightment
In seeing all new they are filled with excitement
By spending our time in the presence of those
The blossoming saplings, the tiniest Rose
It fills us with joy, with a sense of such fun
Remembering back to when we were young
As fully grown blooms we work ourselves, so
Forgetting that play is a way to let go
Join in the garden with daisies, make chains
Run round a meadow and dance in the rain
Talk to the fairies, play, make believe
Have fun and be grateful for all you receive

The Night Rose

The Rose, she lays her weary head
Upon her pillowed softest bed
She nestles in her soil filled nest
Her leaves, they rustle, then they rest
The brush of moonlight, soothing deep
She drifts in dreamless, peaceful sleep

The Climbing Rose

The Rose where she lies has the highest of view
Wrapped in the warmth of the Sun, high she grew
Watching below all her flowers with care
Sending them love and her nurture for e'er
Hoping at night when they're tucked up in bed
They'll catch her sweet fragrance whilst resting their heads
She'll bend down to reach them to give them a kiss
In hope they receive just a taste of her bliss
So, in their Rose garden, they'll reach to the sky
Then, like her flower, they'll raise just as high

The Withering Rose

The Rose in her bed is beginning to age
Accepting her fate as she turns the next page
Her scent still it flows though her petals may fall
Her stem just as strong, she is graceful and tall
She flows with the time, no need to stop clocks
When her last petal falls her sweet fragrance will stop
She knows that her flowers will be born again
Then rests in the moment with no thought to then
For true love is ageless, no time in the heart
The Rose and the Sun they are never apart

The Rambling Rose

She wanders the earth, she travels the land
She lifts others up by taking their hand
She rambles and climbs the steepest of heights
Her journey of love; destination in sight
She creeps, and she crawls giving love to all those
That cross on the path of the rambling Rose

The Frosted Rose

The Rose within her winter bed
She shivers; frost it tips her head
She tries to lift it, feeling bold
So weighed down by the icy cold
She knows the Sun will come to thaw
Her frosted petals like before
Still in her icy bed she sings
She knows the Sun will shine in spring

The Softest Rose

The softest Rose, a gentle bloom
Anger, she does not consume
For if another Rose throws mud
She gazes closely at its bud
She sees the bud, it throws from pain
So if she throws it back again
It covers all with thickest dirt
The muddy pain will then all hurt
And so, she keeps it deep inside
Her petals she will open wide
Compassion sends, to heal the wound
So, they will sing a happy tune
For no one flings around their mud
If they're a truly happy bud

The Lamenting Rose

The Rose in her bed sings a song of lament
Some days she is sad, her stem tired and bent
She knows that the Sun is far up in the sky
Some days she struggles to stretch up that high
And so she will rest as her petals all drop
Awaiting the moment for her sadness to stop
And then she will reach with all of her might
For true love exists at the greatest of heights

The Hardy Rose

The hardy Rose with roots dug deep
As winter comes, her garden sleeps
Her petals long ago she dropped
This time she rests, this time she stops
She slumbers in the frosted garden
Her heart still soft, it never hardens
So still, until she wakes for spring
In rest her strength is gathering
Enduring the hardest of the frosts
The winter snow as soft as dust
Sprinkled gently upon her floor
The coldness causing pain no more
She knows that spring is ever near
In winter nothing she will fear
The seasons come, the cycles turn
In each a lesson she will learn
So in her garden she stands strong
Knowing it is not for long

In summertime her buds will flower
It soon approaches hour by hour
For now she loves the winter snow
She wraps up warm and lets all go
She sees all seasons have their game
Without them all would be the same
And so she nestles in her bed
To rest her weary frosty head

The Grounded Rose

The Rose deeply roots in the earth far below
So grateful for all, for this life here to grow
On earth she is given a garden, a form
Created from the source of the light of the dawn
The more that she worships the light of her source
She surrenders, allowing it to guide her on course
She grows ever stronger, her stem stretches high
Remaining in peace as she touches the sky

The Ever-Present Rose

The Rose when settled in her bed
She never frets her flowering head
With thoughts of what is yet to come
What should or should not have been done
Each moment gone, each second passed
All times before, not meant to last
Uncertain what the future brings
She wastes no time upon these things
But, settles safely in her view
Of budding flowers with hope anew
Enjoying each moment filled with joy
She knows her time is a precious toy

The Morning Rose

The Rose in the morning is covered in dew
Awaiting the sight of her favourite view
Her dewy drops fall, lifts her head for his kiss
In anticipation, in the highest of bliss
For each morn she wakes she is so full of praise
The sight of the Sun and the touch of its rays
Her love for the Sun is her reason to live
And so she cries tears for the love that it gives

The Singing Rose

The Rose as she soaks up the Sun's brightest rays
She never forgets and lowers her gaze
Always she stretches with burning desire
To reach greatest heights so she ever aims higher
Never complacent or settles for less
The Sun is the highest, it brings her the best
She lays in her bed, singing songs full of love
Feeling her heart reaching great heights above

The Compassionate Rose

The Rose with her petals wide open, she sings
At times crosses nettles with harsh words that sting
They bite out with anger, they prickle and crawl
Her heart it keeps singing, her stem standing tall
Though she may feel hurt by the words that they say
She stands strong in silence, and soaks up the rays
For those in the garden who smother and sting
Are acting from places of their suffering
She deeply breathes sunlight, then sends them her scent
For she knows in truth that no harm is meant

Swaying Rose

The Rose in her bed as she sways in the breeze
With wrong kind of care will develop disease
If left without water or feed she will die
No matter how much she will reach to the sky
Her leaves become mottled, they wither and fade
Her stem becomes brown, will need propping and aid
But with the right care she will flourish and grow
Her pure fragrance strong, her petals will glow
Be careful of how you look after a Rose
Her fragrance is sweetest and with nurture it flows

The Peaceful Rose

The Rose when she wakens so warm in her bed
She stretches her stem with such peace in her head
Observing from heights at the chaos around
The garden has problems in beds on the ground
The weeds may invade and the vines try to smother
The ramblers take over, the ground they will cover
She knows in her garden she won't join the fight
She touches the Sun and she fills with its light
She sends from her heart through her roots to the earth
Intending that seeds of her love will be birthed
For all are connected by roots in the ground
The love that she sends in all will be found

The Evolving Rose

Each day you will learn just a little, evolve
Like the softest of petals they slowly unfold
As they open in stillness their scent is released
Bringing within you a longing for peace
This peace it will come when you stop and allow
The sunlight to fill you, be present in now
Opening petals to take in the rays
You'll find yourself growing some more every day
Releasing your fragrance just like the pure Rose
For she is the highest of love that we know

The Neglected Rose

The Rose without some nurture
Without tending, without care
Finds her leaves will slowly crumble
She will gasp for freshest air
She looks into other gardens
Where they're watered every day
Rooted in her flower garden
All she does is sit and pray
She will ask the clouds for water
So her leaves and roots can drink
She will look up at the sunshine
Before her final petals shrink
For the Rose without her nurture
Without tender loving care
She will slowly die and wither
In the garden we all share
She surrenders to the sunshine
To the clouds and to the rain

Hoping they will give her water
And she'll find her love again

The Finest Rose

The Rose is aware of all that she needs
Receives only finest, the highest of feed
Rejecting poor quality from her rose bed
Her roots are deserving the best, so she's fed
To fill her with energy, free from disease
The best of nutrition, she flowers with ease
Her roots they grow strong, and soon she will thrive
So feed her with love to keep her alive

The Gazing Rose

The Rose, though gazing at the skies
No other flower she denies
She fills with sunlight from above
So she can share her endless love
She stretches high but roots down low
To earth's great centre deep below
Her roots give strength if storms may come
They hold her whilst she fills with the Sun
Then from her petals she will start
To share from the eternal heart

The Stretching Rose

The Rose as she rises, as she stretches and yawns
Awake with the sunlight, awake with the dawn
She knows, as she stretches high up as she yearns
The Sun will not scorch her, the light will not burn
Her love sees her reaching and sends down its rays
To touch her pure heart, it is purest love's way
The Rose gives her heart, but she also receives
Pure love fills her all, petals, roots, stems, and leaves

The Wild Rose

As the Rose unfolds her petals to greet the Sun at dawn
You will notice only five which open slowly in the morn
Every petal gives a clue as to how we're formed on earth
All the elements in nature used to form our sacred birth
There are clues within the petals, there are clues within the skies
All this knowledge known by ancients, once again on earth they rise
For they saw her all in nature, her creation all around
How she birthed us such a heaven, we reside on hallowed ground

The Wild Rose

CHAPTER 2

THE ROSE GARDEN

Resting in the Garden

I want to rest in a garden
Where the flowers are always in bloom
Where the sun light is forever
Shining with its energising rays
Where the mountain springs
The clear oceans and rivers
Cleanse the land with its dewy rain
I awaken each morning
To only the sound of birdsong
Where the airs are clear and buzzing
With wildlife, insects humming
Hurrying and flurrying
Where the earth is filled with nutrients to feed all
The flowers grow wild, the herbs grow
The trees stretch their limbs in celebration
This is the vision for my garden

Variety in the Garden

In the garden of the Rose
With its many blooming flowers
Of such colours, size, and fragrance
I could stare at them for hours
As I gaze around the garden
Taking in each one's own beauty
Knowing all will have its place
Each one carrying out its duty
For each flower has its roots
Buried deep within the soil
None is better than another
No more worthy or more royal
For each will slowly blossom
Some more quickly, some take time
There's no rush in nature's garden
For they all are doing fine
In each flower lies deep beauty
Blending perfectly as one

Growing timely in their garden
Under love's eternal Sun

The Tale of a Rose

I woke up in a garden
Feeling the kiss of the Sun on my petals
Stretching my stem upwards I rose
Grateful for the warmth …
Looking around me there were an army of weeds invading my blooms
I built myself a fortress of thorns and slowly they crept away
Still, they remained in my garden
Glancing at their leaves, they appeared as ugly as I was beautiful
I looked up at the sky and then I only saw clouds
The heavens broke and the rain poured down on me
I cried in the rain watching the drops falling onto the mother beneath me and she sent me her love through my roots
As the rain eased the wind spoke to the clouds who drifted apart and let in the Sun

Drying in its rays I noticed a rainbow
As I gazed at it, I heard sobbing from the weeds as they were in the shade
I remembered they were a plant just like me
I drew back my thorns and lowered my defences
I whispered to the wind, and he sent them my fragrance
He blew with all his might and the clouds disappeared
As they breathed in my scent, they received my sweet fragrance
They dried their tears as the Sun shone down and lit up their petals
They realised there was enough nourishment in the soil for us all
Opening their newly birthed buds to the Sun they welcomed in the rain
No longer looking to compete for space I finally saw their beauty
Together in our garden we grew

My Garden Within

There is peace in my garden
Of dandelions and roses
Not bothered by the wilderness
Of ivy and poppies
Of old curled up hoses

There is peace in my garden
The rustling of grasses
Undisturbed by the breezes
The edges and the hedges
Bordering on unkempt

There is peace in my garden
With pots needing haircuts
Rusty tables and chairs
Withered old daffodils
Now sleeping 'til spring

There is peace in my garden
The insects a scurrying
Hurrying and worrying
Butterflies a flitting
From blossom to bloom

There is peace in my garden
Counting petals, making wishes
Hearing birdsong from branches
My garden a paradise
My garden within

Bind Weed

In the depths of the garden slowly creeping so mild
In the darkest of corners she takes over left wild
Her leaves are intrusive, she tries hard to bind
When left suffocating as she twists and she winds
But if she's cut back and she's under control
She can stay in the garden within her earth role
Ignored and not tended she'll stay overgrown
She'll cover like blankets, the flowers will moan
Acknowledge the weed but don't let it bind
Remember it’s there as it's spreading, unwind
For if you keep checking it soon finds its place
The Rose is then free left to breathe in her space

The Herb Garden

The Rose in her garden, her warm cosy bed
So sleepy surrounded by lavender heads
For she is another with such healing power
Her qualities soothing to sleep hour by hour
She has many neighbours, the jasmine so sweet
Exchanging their fragrance, her scent is a treat
The sage, she is cleansing, she soothes like a balm
Grateful for chamomile, cooling and calm
The healing herb garden, aromas all blend
They share their sweet fragrance, with love all they send
They share all they're gifted, each other they shower
In love's purest garden, all have healing power

Jasmine Bloom

With whitest flowers that bloom at night
The modest jasmine a purest sight
The heady scent of petals pearly
The sensual fragrance awakens early
Two sleeping lovers entwined as one
To greet the early morning Sun

The Sunflower

The Rose in her garden so pleased with her view
She watches, observes anything that is new
The sunflowers blooming with huge beaming smiles
That raise all our spirits, they lift up for miles
The happiest bloom in the garden so dear
Just born with the purest of joy, this is clear
The moment their seedling is dropped in the bed
They're plotting and planning to raise their great heads
They can't wait to greet the sky's glorious Sun
They wriggle and wiggle, the prospect such fun
They sprout up their shoots, their stems grow so tall
The largest of heads and the highest of all
The giants of flowers, the Rose she smiles wide
For how can you frown with the Sun at your side?

The Lotus

The lotus, a flower that starts as a bud
Still closed in the depths of the grime and the mud
For her flower to blossom in murkiest pools
She has to make way to the light that is full
She spies through the algae, the sludge and the weed
The shimmery surface of watery beads
Climbing, she yearns for the surface so bright
Her goal is to open to shimmering light
She breaks through the layers of watery mud
Opening petals, her beautiful bud
In bloom she emerges her flower now whole
For reaching the light of the Sun is her goal

The Lily Pond

The Rose in her garden, one part she is fond
Are the lilies of many that float in her pond
A rainbow of colours, so pretty to see
She sits at the edge and she watches with glee
She sees a dear frog from each colour it hops
It checks each is healthy, he pauses, he stops
Cleaning each lily if bound fast with weed
Or floating off course, to be clear all they need
He hops to another, and each gives a glow
Afloat and strong stemmed, deeply rooted below
When he is happy with each in his sight
He hops to the largest, the lily of white
Her one thousand petals unfold, and they shine
The sight of her flower the purest Divine
The Rose in the highest of peace by her pond
In moments of stillness she goes far beyond

Garden Maintenance

In Love's Divine Garden the Rose does her best
To keep her bed tidy and not leave a mess
She looks all around her and wonders at times
If the reason she's tired is the weeds and the vines
For if these are left to go wild and to grow
They make her feel tired, and her energy goes
She maintains her garden and keeps it all clear
So she's not overwhelmed by the weeds every year

Surrender to Nature

The Rose in her garden content in her bed
Surrenders to nature, allows to be led
She digs her roots deeply for a water supply
If there is no rain, on some days it is dry
She digs even deeper on days of high winds
She knows it will pass, she has faced harder things
When elements batter with hail or with snow
She stands strong and grounded, she knows it will go
For nature it brings a diverse weather set
Each day in her garden she accepts what she gets

The Bee

The Rose while lying in her bed
She knows the bee, her nectar spreads
She doesn't force the bees to come
In waiting still she hears their hum
Her blooms in flower open wide
Her fragrance draws a bee inside
It takes its feed on nectar sweet
Then pollinates each flower it meets
This is the way in which she shares
Her honey fragrance with all there

Synergy

The Rose as she rests in her garden, her ground
She likes to observe all the goings around
The sunflowers smiling, the chamomile, calm
The lavender sleepy, they stretch and they yawn
Some seedlings are pushing their way through her bed
She gives them her fragrance, they need to be fed
She nods to the sage, the wisest of herbs
His fragrance so cleansing, his purpose to serve
The elegant lilies, the tall hollyhocks
Bring joy to the wildlife, the insects they flock
Each flower, each insect, each herb has a task
They give with abundance and nothing they ask
They tend to their garden with love and with care
Respect one another, there's plenty to share
The Rose full of love she observes all of this
Then sends out her fragrance in thanks with a kiss

The Frog

The frog as it swims to the murkiest depths
Finds joy in the water and peace on the steps
The surface, the water, the pads of the lilies
It wonders why those in the pond are so silly
They never find peace in the stillness and calm
So scared of the water, they'll come to no harm
For a frog on a lily, he dives down and swims
No water is murky enough to stop him
For the water it feeds him, the air gives him breath
He uses both aspects, both light and then depth

The Bat

She dances, spins on dusky skies
She flits with grace before my eyes
A serenade, the swiftest song
In darkest nights where she belongs
Her nest, it lies in rooftops high
In twilight swirls in velvet sky
Her presence clear, in silent flight
The bat, the guardian of the night

The Robin

He sat by my side and he sang me a song
A sonnet, a gift, of how we all belong
He sat by my side and he called out my name
He opened my heart, freed of all guilt and shame
He sat by my side and he gave me a lift
The greatest of presents, greatest of gift
He sat by my side just to give me a call
A message of love so I gift this to all

The Spider

The spider in weaving her intricate web
So engrossed in her work, is not lost or misled
The web it is spun from the finest of silk
Each one spun before from a similar ilk
She spins like the cosmos, evolves and expands
It grows as she weaves from her small spider hands
Each intricate move she will perfectly spin
Like the way we're created, how all life begins

A Taste of Nectar

The bee as it buzzes so close to the Rose
In merriment hums as it follows its nose
It smells the sweet nectar from outside the flower
Drawn in by the fragrance then drinks in its power
A taste of the honey in the Rose's pure heart
The bee is now silent whilst lost in his art
When finished no buzzing, a serene little sound
A soft little hum as it's flying around
The taste of the nectar of purest Divine
The essence of honey, like finest of wine
Can calm all the buzzing, the noise of debate
Gives peace in the soul to just be and vibrate
For once you have tasted the nectar you seek
There's no need to question and no need to speak

Fragrance

The fragrance, the nectar that comes from the flower
Is what gives the insects their mightiest power
No worries to enter the holiest room
That they may be trapped in her sticky, sweet bloom
They fly in regardless, they hover and drink
So drunk on her fragrance they've no time to think
They guzzle in ecstasy, drink 'til they're filled
Then fly to their nest where they settle so still

The Willow

The willow with its leaves of tears
Its saddened branches drip in lakes
To soften hearts that huddle sheltered
Comforting their fond mistakes

The willow weeping with compassion
Dripping tears of empathy
Its limbs embrace those souls who shelter
Needing deepest sympathy

The willow with its arms of shelter
Gripped in its embrace of care
Sobs so softly on the breeze
You'd barely notice it was there

The Nightingale

The Nightingale with song of beauty
Her call to all her only duty
Her melody so sweet and high
Her tune her own with wings she flies
To cage her is the greatest sin
With bars and locks, her suffering
Unlock the cage and watch her soar
She'll sing to you forever more
In purest song her voice will raise
And lead you all to better days

Weaving the Web

The Rose in her bed with her fill of the Sun
She watches a spider, her web she has spun
So busy creating such beauty today
Observing its spinning to lure in its prey
It glistens and shimmers with silk it has sheen
So fast with her weaving, just like a machine
She knows that its purpose is here just to weave
To catch in its prey, so then it can feed
She knows this her nature, she knows this is so
She watches in peace from her bed down below
The spider whose beautiful weaving is done
Will feast on its prey in its web it has spun

Beauty In the Night

The Rose sees beauty in the night
She gazes at the stars so bright
She makes a wish upon a star
And sends it true love from afar
For galaxies so vast, so wide
So blessed this cannot be denied
Our universe goes far beyond
Our earthly land, our sacred pond
Amongst the stars this tiny earth
The Rose is honoured for her birth

A Bed of Roses

The Rose as she stretches great heights full of praise
For all in her garden, they help her to raise
The flowers who struggle with finding their Sun
Still sending their fragrance to raise everyone
Their hearts full of love, they just wish to please
They live to give scent to the flowers and trees
At times they may tire, their heady scent fades
Fatigued, curl their petals to energy save
With rest they can fill with the Sun's golden light
Topped up with sweet fragrance, their blooms shining
bright

We are like birds that are always soaring through this infinite sky singing our story of love. We may pass through the realm of death, but we keep on singing. We begin a new verse of our song soaring to greatest heights, our song heard by all. Forever singing.

Forever Singing

A nightingale, she sings her song
Her tune it passes far and long
A song of love will never fade
For greatest heights its notes are made
Her song is an eternal tune
It never dies, through death resumes
It sweetly sings another verse
The nightingale, her call on earth
Through all existence, time and state
Her purest song through all vibrates

Dispersing Mists

Some mornings in the garden
There will lie a heavy fog
It is hard to want to waken
When surrounded by a smog
But the mists will soon disperse
When the sunlight hits the clouds
With its warmth it soon evaporates
Releases from its shroud
So if all seems thick and foggy
Always focus on the Sun
Know its warmth and shining rays
Are always there, will always come
For in nature's purest garden
Fogs will come and they will go
Sunlight always raises mists
Revealing all that's real to show

Darkest of Night

The Rose as she lies in the darkest of night
Gives thanks to each star as it's shining so bright
She smiles at the moon as it lights up the sky
It gives her some comfort in her bed where she lies
But although each star and the moon tries its best
She knows it's still night in the bed where she rests
She waits for her lover, the Sun in the morn
Night only will go when Sun rises at dawn

Opium Hearts

She is eternal, the love that she brings
Her scent fills the garden, each blossom it sings
The poppies they shimmer, their opium hearts
The fragrance of summer, the pollen it darts
She feeds all, she loves all, her magic she plants
All under her spell of such beauty, entranced
For nothing can break the pure hearts of lovers
The Rose and the Sun, divine father, and mother

CHAPTER 3

ROSE

CARE

Sacred Bath

Within my sacred bath of Rose
With soapy bubbles filled
I find you bathing by my side
Washing away my ills
Together we will clean and bathe
Until I'm purest light
And then we'll float above all waves
On stormiest of nights
With sacred oils we both anoint
With blessing so we raise
Forever in our sacred bath
Our soapy warm embrace

Presence

Our greatest gift is in the now
Our present moment shows us how
There is no future or no past
This moment now will ever last
Be mindful of all on our ground
The miracle of life astounds
The beauty of a fragrant flower
The wonders of creation's power
It humbles us in gratitude
Can help us change our attitude
For nothing else we need, the gift
Our life on earth, it gives a lift
For all we see is made with love
We're forged from something high above
In each of us we all are one
A part of life's eternal Sun

Gratitude

When the Rose awakes each morning
Rising up beside the Sun
As she opens her first petal
Pausing, takes in everyone
She will look around her garden
Giving thanks to all around
Some still sleeping ever peaceful
Soft and gentle on the ground
In her stillness and her gratitude
Such joy she feels inside
Full of energy and love for all
Her petals open wide

Higher Focus

A Rose as she awaits the moon
No focus on the doom and gloom
She doesn't listen to the talk
The gossip other flowers talk
She sends her fragrance far and wide
In stillness deepens, goes inside
And bathes in moonlight from her bed
Not letting others fill her head
Just focusing on love's pure light
Before she rests another night

Sowing the Seeds

When sowing our seeds of love, when we scatter
Without spreading muck, for hearts it will shatter
With water and nurture, with Sun shining bright
Conditions for growing must always be right
Watching with joy as our seed starts to sprout
From firm roots they surface, then leaves and shoots
spout
We give them our time and our tenderest care
So one day they bloom from the love that we share

Rose Wisdom

The Rose as she opens her petals, each one
In raising her bloom to her lover, the Sun
Expands in her wisdom, her knowledge it blooms
Her fragrance grows stronger to fill every room
For in her pure presence she fills all with peace
They stop, and they take in the scent she's released
Revealing herself to the world for a while
Then folds up her petals to rest with a smile

Watering the Garden

The Rose within her garden always reaching for the Sun
With her ever-growing blossoms sending fragrance to
each one
She looks around her garden with a softness in her gaze
Her garden lit with sunlight; in each flower, sees its rays
In opening her petals with her head raised high above
She notices her fragrance is the same as purest love
For sunlight in the garden is the ray that fills each flower
By giving it our focus we are drenched with sunlit
shower
Purest love is its vibration like the fragrance of the Rose
We allow its love to fill us as we're watered with its hose

Rose-tinted Glasses

I see through eyes of a glass tinted Rose
For many a view that they wish to oppose
How can you see there is true love in all?
We come in this world with a light very small
A spark, oh so tiny, in all it will grow
If nurtured with care and with loving to show
For all, they will have this deep hidden spark
But without some nurture, it is hidden by dark
By seeing this truth in each one with compassion
You soon see the reason behind every action
You may not approve of some things they have done
But we have no knowledge of how they begun
We're not here on earth to judge and condemn
We're here to share love to each one, to all men

Preparing Her Bed

The Rose that is free can rewrite her own story
She lifts to the Sun and she basks in its glory
The stories that planted her bed with bad seeds
Are soon taken out when she sees they are weeds
For there is no place for those tales in her bed
She writes all her own with the words in her head
The seeds that she plants she gives time to each day
She watches them grow in the warm sunlit rays
With nurture they bloom and she watches with pride
For heaven on earth is where she resides

Lost in the Garden

In the Rose's sunlit garden there is sometimes dropped a seed
It will take some time to settle as it nestles down to feed
But the tiniest of seedling as it starts to feed and grow
Can feel lost within the garden as its flowers start to show
For it's nothing like the flowers, in the garden, in this space
As it gazes on the others it feels different, out of place
But the Rose with her perception holds a mirror to this bloom
Asks it just to peer inside, let go of feelings that consume
As it peers inside her mirror with surprise it sees a sight
One of greatest, highest beauty, of the purest source of light
For each flower in the garden has a fragrance sweet inside

We all have it deep within us from the source in all resides
Every flower in the garden, every weed will have a place
There is so much room to grow when we see beauty in each face
Sometimes we need a mirror to be held up by the Rose
We see our true reflection, it never lies, the truth it shows

Garden Design

I fashion my world as I wish to portray
Create an appearance, a lovely display
I think very clearly what I wish to see
In my perfect garden, I choose carefully
What seeds I disperse to water and sow
The highest ideas I plant deep below
I wish for my garden to have every hue
To brighten the beds for the lovelies view
I sprinkle with water and magical feed
To nourish the flowers in beds as they seed
I know my creation is how it should be
For all that is growing is planted by me

Pottering

The Rose in her garden she helps to create
She doesn't lie dormant, she participates
For though she has love for the Sun in her heart
She knows in her garden they're never apart
She raises her head as she potters in fun
Aware of the heat she can feel from the Sun
It gives her such strength as she works every day
She feels it in tasks and she feels it in play
At night when she rests, she reflects on the sky
The stars in the darkness, she watches them fly
So happy her garden, so perfect around
She knows she is blessed on this holiest ground

Planting Seeds

The Rose in her garden takes time to reflect
Allowing the brightest of Sun to inject
By sunlight of dawn in dhyana and praise
She clears her vibration, allows this to raise
Aware that each thought that she plants is a seed
So chooses which ones to give time to and feed
She knows being mindful of how she vibrates
Will bring in the same, this is how she creates
In her warm sacred bed she brings miracles in
So grateful for all, this is how it begins
For all is vibration, the spiritual laws
She sets good intentions, no focus on flaws
She sows, and she reaps, she receives what she gives
She creates her own vision that she wants to live

Focus

The Rose remains focused, the storms they do come
She strengthens her roots, still she stares at the Sun
For nothing can stop her averting her gaze
The wind it may howl but her head she keeps raised
She may lose some leaves, her petals may fall
Her stem remains strong as she stretches up tall
Her scent never fades, her heart never dies
For pure Divine Love all she feels where she lies

Rose Light

Where is Love in a world that is dual?
So hard to remember on our earthly school
In highest, Divine, in its true perfect form
The lowest is hate that can leave us forlorn
It manifests here in so many great ways
The love of a mother, a friendship, a gaze
The lust for a lover, a burning desire
In truth we are searching for something much higher
Devotion to others can help us reach heights
Of love never realised by changing our sight
As soon as you see through the glasses of Rose
You see love in all and your purest heart grows

Strong Roots

The Rose with her pure fragrance
With her thorns so sharp and strong
She has everything she needs
In her bed where she belongs
Still she's ever looking upwards
To the warmth she feels above
To the source that ever feeds her
To her one eternal love
She gives thanks for all she has
In her bed she does not cling
For love and bliss eternal
Only sunlight this will bring

Contentment

The Rose as she awakens in the morning to the Sun
She arises feeling grateful that another day's begun
She knows that all she does in nature's garden is Divine
Her path is full of grace, she allows and she will shine
Each action that she does is always filled with joy and
love
All does is out of service for the Sun that shines above
Every morning she awakens bringing sunlight to her
heart
So she can share her fragrance as the day begins to start

Self-Love

The Rose with her love for the Sun is so real
It emanates all that she sees and she feels
She knows that the source of her love is inside
It lies deep within and in all it resides
It nourishes all and it gives so much bliss
It's why she keeps reaching so high with a kiss
It feeds her, it lifts her, brings back to her health
She knows purest love resides in her Self

Higher Focus

The Rose on the Sun, always steady her gaze
Her focus remains and forever it stays
For here in her garden distractions will come
But nothing will take her away from the Sun
She sets her gaze highest though always aware
The garden around her with problems are there
She trusts when she focuses highest her mind
Solutions will come, with ease she will find
Her love keeps her strong, her trust in the Sun
With love and devotion all will overcome

Busy doing Nothing

The Rose in her garden she stares at the sky
She watches the clouds as they softly drift by
She feels on her petals the gentlest breeze
Aware in the distance the hum of the bee
She catches the scent of her neighbouring flowers
With all of these senses she's busy for hours
With nothing to do but to feel, sense and hear
Content in her bed full of blessings so dear

Scattering Seeds

Never stop dreaming or planting your seeds
Your wishes come true on the scope of your deeds
Some will grow blooms and some will grow weeds
All part of the garden, the fruit of the trees
No need to be selfish and focus on greed
Or expect a harvest at greatest of speed
The seeds that you scatter with highest of feed
Will grow in the future to all that you need

New Petals

The Rose she sheds her final petal
She sits and waits for all to settle
Waiting for the morning rays
To bring forth new and better days
For she can shed no petals more
She's not defined by those before
The dawn awaits, new petals come
This time they're golden like the Sun

Weeding the Garden

In Love's pure Garden the Rose may find
Around her roots some weeds may bind
They've buried in the soil and clay
She pulls them out and throws away
But if she just destroys their tops
They'll soon grow back, they'll never stop
They try to suffocate her stem
Her leaves grow weak, she suffers then
And so she digs them from the roots
To stop their growth, to stop their shoots
Then she can clearly breathe again
Replenished by the Sun and rain

Shade

The Rose when she has no shade from the Sun
Her petals may fade or crumble, each one
For sometimes the brightness is too much to bear
A cover of shade gives her tenderest care
For shadow and sunlight the balance she needs
In her garden to thrive and to plant her new seeds

Shedding Petals

The Rose in the garden, the bed where she slept
She dropped all her petals, they spilled as she wept
For looking around her the clumps of sweet flowers
Grew up all together to give them more power
But wouldn't allow one another to spread
They stayed far apart in a different bed
They thought they were beautiful, more than the rest
So stuck with their crowd, they were holy and blessed
She saw just a garden of beautiful flowers
Each different, she gazed at their beauty for hours
But saddened to see such divide all around
So left all her petals to drift on the ground

Rose in Meditation

Let's take a pause and connect with the Sun
Feel the Rose in your heart, she's in all, everyone
Unlock every petal to open full bloom
Feel them softly revealing the heart, love consumes
As you open, the sunlight will fill you inside
The source of your bliss, in your heart will reside

Rose in our Hearts

The Rose in our hearts, as her petals unfold
She opens the gateway to speak to our soul
As purest Love pours, as it flows out and in
Her softest pink ray fills us up from within
As we open our petals, our inner light shines
The Rose is a portal to our Self Divine

Gardening

The Rose though focused on the Sun
There's garden work that must be done
Before she rests her sleepy head
There's seeds to sow and clear her bed
She looks up high and gives her praise
Fills up with love then sets her gaze
On tasks she has, the here and now
She carries on to sow and plough

Losing Sight

The Rose at times she loses sight
By all the garden noise at night
Forgets to focus on the Sun
Her focus turns to everyone
She wishes all her garden bliss
That they could feel the Sun's pure kiss
She soon remembers love is there
For all to know, for all to share
Within the stillness, not in sound
It is not gifted, must be found
And so she stretches up her shoots
Deep in the earth she sends her roots
She lifts her head in highest bliss
As she receives a sunlit kiss

The Heart of the Rose

The Rose appears she's ever strong
Her thorns are hard, her stem is long
Her petals soft against your cheek
Her fragrance gentle, mild and meek
Her outer stance will keep her safe
Below the surface lies her grace
For when she opens her flowers to you
You'll see a shining heart that's true

CHAPTER 4

TALES OF A ROSE

Briar Rose

Aurora, she slept for one hundred years
Her family wept, shed thousands of tears
In a faraway land, her fragrance it drifted
To a handsome young Prince, by her scent, he felt lifted
Asleep in a castle surrounded by thorns
For true love he battled, dark magic he scorned
Awakened one day by the kiss of Divine
She opened her eyes, their hearts now entwined
Together united, the magic they froze
All from the scent of a beautiful Rose

A Mystical Rose

There once was a maid, a mystical rose
Awoken one day with the gift of sweet prose
She'd never once written a singular line
But gifted her heart to her true love Divine
From that moment onwards all flowed was her love
Of heavenly moments from below and above
In seeking to show her true feelings inside
It opened a new world, her heart opened wide
The presence it gifted her gave her pure bliss
All from the brush of the tenderest kiss

St Theresa of Avilla

The path of a mystic
A solitary way
A pavement for one
With Love guiding each day
A mystical Rose
Found love deep inside
Within a vast mansion
Her journey resides
In seven soul chambers
Through which she did travel
The journey through each
Love's mysteries unravel
We're each on a journey
Some mystical minds
Which ever your path
Just let it unwind

Melissa

I drip my sweet nectar upon your soft toes
Breathe in my pure essence, the scent of the Rose
For I am the priestess of honey, the bee
A virgin Melissa, in your temple find me

Alice

Curiouser and Curiouser. Down the rabbit hole we fly only to wake up when we smell the Roses in the garden of the Queen of Hearts

Down the rabbit hole she flew
If only then she really knew
The journey she was soon to start
Would finish with the Queen of Hearts
The only way back up she knows
Is following the fragrant Rose

Myrraphore

From my garden of the Rose
I gather sweetest flowers
The delicate of fragrance
With petals I will shower

Steeped in purest oils
A scent from holy earth
Breathe it in, the deepest bliss
Your happiness I birth

With this sacred Rose
Of oil anoint I bless
Feel kisses on your crown
Within her arms you rest

The Rose of the East – Quan Yin

The Rose of compassion from far eastern shores
Enlightened, but hearing our call came once more
For although she rose the highest, ascended
She knew that on earth she was needed, depended
With love and compassion, she inspires all
To open our petals, to stretch up so tall

Eden

The Rose is a symbol of eternal Love
The sign of Divine, all within not above
The Rose she resides in the garden, in all
Our garden of Eden, Sophia did fall
The snake it was winding up our tree of life
Shiva and Shakti, the husband and wife
Or Adam and Eve, the Sophia and Christ
Their names do not matter, they soon will unite
For when true love Rose and then became one
Entwined in the arms of the eternal Sun
Two lovers created a heaven on earth
His seed in her womb of true Love, a rebirth

Off with her head!

Alice in wonderland wondering, wandering
In such a quandary of questioning, pondering
Following rabbits in such a mad rush
The tea party, never she could find a hush
The bottles for drinking, the cake she could eat
Adapting and changing is such a real feat
She grew and she grew, she outgrew a house
There cropped up the smallest of voices, a mouse
She carried on searching, her way out a must
In so many creatures she'd given her trust
She found a Rose Garden and "Off with her head"
So frightened she feared that the Queen wished her dead
In this very moment was when she awoke
The fear for her life from the Queen that she spoke
In searching, adventuring on her path she roamed
She soon found herself and she knew she was home

The Secret of the Rose

The Rose fast asleep in her deep rooted bed
The deepest of crimson, her beauteous head
We know she was wakened by her true love's kiss
The Prince, in the tales awakening bliss
As she starts to grow then her colours soon shift
She winds and she spirals through a rainbow she lifts
For the Rose is the serpent in our root we will find
Awakened from slumber she starts to unwind
At the end of the rainbow there lies molten gold
The secret of the Rose in her bed now unfolds

Breaking the Spell

The Rose as she lies fast asleep
Her crimson lips with roots so deep
So unaware for her to wake
From her enchantment, love can break
The purest kiss alone will prise
Her from her slumber and arise
For only when two join as one
They lift together to the Sun
The serpent wakes, uncoils, alert
It sheds its skin upon the dirt
She lifts the Rose with bravest Knight
Back to their home of greatest heights
The spell is broken, rising free
Together for eternity

The Red Queen

The Queen, she tended Roses
In her garden full of care
When entered poor old Alice
With her band of blue in her hair
She offered her such pleasure
Inside the garden of the heart
Enjoy her new surroundings
Even offered tea and tarts
But always Alice worried
On her search for home she cried
“Off with her head” such wisdom
The Queen of Hearts, she tried
For Alice had forgotten
In her wonderland of thoughts
Her heart will guide her, show the way
To find the place she sought
By being in the garden
Smelling roses, playing

Her search for home, her journey

It would never be the same

The Crowned Rose

I am the eye, I see it all
The Rose is crowned
She stands so tall
Upon the sands of Egypt climbs
To bring the heavens down Divine
Between the Sun and moon you reach
The point eternal that you seek
The eye of Horus, Horus eye
Look deep within for truth you spy

Bringers of the Rose

The warriors of love they sing
They waltz the cosmic dance
They came to earth on mother's call
To all around enhance
The carriers of mother wound
The medals that they earned
No longer scarred or terrorised
Filled with the love they yearned
For they are bringers of the Rose
She rises in the depths
They feel her cosmic dance within
In balance with their breath
So, in these times of mother's call
The healers stand, arise
For they will reap the fruits of love
The highest of a prize

CHAPTER 5

SEASONS

&

CYCLES

The Budding Rose

A Rose, she begins as the tiniest bud
She pushes her shoots from the darkest of mud
With greatest of strength she will grow over years
It takes all her might and she sheds many tears
She has many nights when she feels so forlorn
Some may try to pluck her so she hardens her thorns
It may seem her growing takes infinite hours
But soon with her focus her buds turn to flowers
For each of us all have the essence of Rose
We find it inside us, with nurture it grows
For all were once buds and with love and with care
We help other flowers by showing we're there

The Hope of Spring

The Rose delights upon the spring
The newest birds, the chorus sings
As chicks are fledging in the dawn
Her frosty bed the soil, now warm
She stretches up her forming buds
Awaits the heat of her true love
And as the chicks take flight with wings
She's full of hope, renewal brings.

The Dawn Chorus

She wakes in the morn
To the dawn chorus call
So peaceful and tranquil
Allows all to fall
Gives thanks for her blessings
The dawn chorus song
Awaits the first glimpse
Of her lover she longs
She let's all her sadness
And suffering go
Surrenders to dawn
She allows all to flow

Another Dawn, Another Day

The Rose arises strong and fast
She sees her garden ever vast
The soft horizon far away
Another dawn, another day
She knows each day brings something new
The drops of rain, the gentle dew
The mists will rise, the Sun will beam
The waters flow, the running stream
For nothing ever stays the same
In every moment a picture frame

Dawn Praise

The Rose she wakens with the dawn
So grateful for the early morn
For this is when she greets the Sun
In peace before the day's begun
In stillness she will sing its praise
For filling her with purest rays
She feels the calm and fills with light
Then rises from her bed so bright
Her petals open, stretched above
With grace she sends all purest love

Mirror of the Sun

A mirror of the Sun
Sweet child of the moon
Your fragrance I hold
The sweetest perfume

In darkness you shine
A beacon in the dark
Your pools of moonlight
Fill my restless heart

I welcome your cycles
Surrender to change
For nothing is stagnant
On the holiest stage

Blessing of the Sun

As the days are the longest
The Sun fills the skies
We fill with deep blessings
As we watch it arise
For here in the dawn
We see happier days
Renewed expectations
From lifting the haze
We move into summer
With all now in bloom
The skies of your warmth
Will fill all of us soon

Mother Rose

I plump the softest pillows
You may softly lay your head
Amongst the soil and leaves you lie
Upon my fragrant bed

I wrap you in my petals
I will take away your fears
Deep in my roots they're washed away
By dewy drops of tears

Sleep my love and let it all
Be taken by the night
Rest your weary petals
Fill your heart with golden light

I’ll cover you with kisses
Let the day just drift away
I’ll hold you in your slumber
Til you rise another day

Call of the Mother

The call of the mother to enter your cave
Retreat in the space where all blessings will save
She places a Rose in the depths of your womb
The petals a thousand, they light up the room
The pain of before that has left you bereft
No longer resides, it long now has left
In highest vibration, the purest of light
The womb of the mother, she holds you so tight

A Rose in Full Bloom

The Rose in soporific love
The existential state above
Arisen in her bed of thorns
No time for hurt or pain or scorn
She flowers on this sacred earth
Her presence reason for her birth
For knowing this and nothing more
Her love flows pure within her pores
Her essence, fragrance, purest oil
Will spread through roots in finest soil

The Wilting Rose

As petals fall from a lonely flower
Her time has reached its final hour
She isn't sad but reaches up
To fill her buds from pure love's cup
For soon she'll blossom once again
She takes her time, we don't know when
But soon she'll bloom, her scent will spread
A Rose never dies in her sacred bed

Fallen Leaves

She sighs on the wind, her shelter the trees
She settles on carpets of soft fallen leaves
She sings her lament for her love so afar
In her soft beating heart there is always a scar
She pictures her love in the carpet of leaves
Remembers his touch in the gentle wind's breeze
She blows him a kiss, sends it up to the stars
So this he can feel from his homeland afar
She smiles in her bed as she touches her heart
His love deep inside, they are never apart

The Mature Rose

The oldest of Roses, the tallest, she towers
She's had many blossoms, an abundance of flowers
She entered the garden as the smallest of buds
She buried her roots in the soil and the mud
She strengthened her tendrils and raised up her head
To drink in the rain and with sunlight was fed
She's seen many seasons, endured many storms
She kept herself raised and she strengthened her thorns
She learnt how to help other rosebuds to grow
Protect from the elements, rain and the snow
She showed them the ways to fill up with the Sun
Reminded them always to smile and have fun
To remember that although the highest above
They still are a flower in the garden of love

Winter Petals

Frozen petals tipped with ice
Still soft to touch but in a trice
They softly drop, a frosty layer
An offering of love, a prayer
Beneath her though a carpet lies
Her love eternal, never dies.

High Winds

Some days in your garden high winds they will come
They try to uproot you but you will stand strong
Your roots are so deep there's strength in your stem
None can unearth you even strongest of men
Some days in your garden dark clouds they will form
They may carry with them the hardest of storms
A storm is expected, its forecast is done
But behind every storm cloud is always the Sun
The Rose in her garden prepares for all weather
She looks to the skies where her love resides ever
She stores up its sunlight for the darkest of days
From this she will feed filled with highest of praise
For though in a storm she may see petals drop
She is forming new buds and her love never stops

Resting Rose

The Rose as she lies in her bed, she is spent
She's grateful for summer, so much merriment
Her petals are falling, she's closing her buds
Wrapped up for some time for herself, some self-love
For being the Rose she is love and is wise
She takes time to rest in the bed that she lies
For autumn and winter the time to restore
She'll rest until spring like each cycle before.

Nature's Cycle

As we enter the season when leaves start to age
Maturing from summer, from youth to a sage
We celebrate harvest of all our supplies
Beginning to slow with a chill in the skies
Storing our wares as we wait for the cold
Reflect and acceptance of our growing old
We see the leaves brittle and snap when they bend
Reminding us everything comes to an end
But all we have stored sees us through to the spring
The cycle continues and new life begins

Ashes to Ashes

Ashes to ashes, dust to dust
From death starts anew, in this we can trust
For even the ashes can nourish and feed
In our earthly garden, our soil it needs
There is no beginning and there is no end
The infinite garden, recycled to tend
The droplets of rain that waters the ground
Evaporates, rises and then forms a cloud
The old rotting petals and leaves in the fall
Go back to the earth and are gifted for all
For there is no waste in the garden of Rose
All goes round in cycles and none is disposed

Restoration

My petals fall in the winter of my love
Awaiting the return of the Sun
Yearning for the warmth of spring
Knowing I will bloom again
'Til then I sleep in the arms of your desire

The Essence of the Rose

The Rose, as her petals are starting to fall
So glad she can feed dearest nature for all
For all that is wilted and shrivelled and dead
Will once again grow in her flowery bed
The light that she stores from her spiritual Sun
Is in every petal and flower, each one
The source of her love, her fragrance won't die
It's in every breathe that we take where we lie
Like petals we wither, grow old and we fade
But never our essence, our fragrance will stay
Returns to the source of our spiritual Sun
Our fragrance it blends with the purest of one

Surrender

The Rose sometimes shelters when winds turn to gales
She closes her petals to rain and to hail
When snow starts to fall she will curl up to rest
She trusts that the elements come as a test
Behind the harsh clouds the Sun still will shine
She knows things are hard but soon will be fine
They say every cloud has a clear silver lining
She doesn't spend time sad and sobbing and pining
For weathers and season all turn like a wheel
But the Sun always shines, she knows this and she feels

Renewal

The Rose in the light of Sun she does swoon
But also finds love in the light of the moon
For sometimes the brightness of Sun it can blind
The moon light and darkness in balance she finds
For she sees the seasons and knows life will flow
The cycle continues with its tos and its fros
In winter her petals will shrivel and die
She takes time to rest in the bed that she lies
Awaits springs renewal, new life, full of hope
The light will return in life's great horoscope

The Cycles of the Rose

The Rose though in love with the highest of Sun
She never forgets all her aspects as one
Allows them to cycle as they lift and rise
She knows many aspects of all will comprise
She knows in the winter her petals will fall
She'll wither and die, she'll curl up in a ball
She moves to the spring with a new sense of love
In summer as mother she gives birth to buds
In autumn prepares yet again for her death
The time of enchantress, her song on her breath
For nothing is linear, the cycle on earth
The mother she spins, she will die then rebirth
To these she surrenders, still focuses high
For though always turning none ever will die
She stands in the middle and watches with care
Sends her scent freely to all that are there

Rose in Battle

The Rose with her flowers is also adorned
With a strong suit of armour for battle, her thorns
For she may be soft like a maiden and mother
She has many aspects you soon will discover
Her petals will fall in the wintery depths
Throughout all the seasons her thorns she has kept
Through cycles of spring and of summer and fall
She'll flourish and grow, and her stem will stand tall
Left on her own she will grow wild and free
She'll prick you with thorns if you won't let her be
Allow her to grow, show her love and your care
Her thorns are so sharp so you'd better beware

Rebirth

The Rose on this day she thanks all the flowers
Reborn in these times to stand in their power
She sees them arising to bring down the light
Bring back the old ways as they stand strong and fight
For she is the goddess, the earth is her place
Her name in the gutter, once slandered, disgraced
The strength of creation has helped her to rise
The men who suppressed her, their time of demise
Once honoured as woman divine and then shamed
For this a rebirth, she is risen again

Creative Fire

Within the garden of the Rose
The space where she inspires my prose
At times I lose creative fire
I gaze around me wilting, tired
I sit and wait, it never lasts
Cycles come, they always pass
Creating new, a poem's birth
In stillness on this sacred earth
Will come from when I gaze above
To feel the rays of purest love

CHAPTER 6

THE SUN

&

THE ROSE

Divine Union

The Sun and the Rose, in balance they meet
In perfect symmetry rest at your feet
Surprising the world with their infinite tie
Their love so sublime it never will die
With surrender to love they rest in embrace
So lost in their moment, no purpose, just grace

Rose Dreams

The Rose from where she drifts and dreams
Awaiting her beloved's beams
The light and tender kiss of light
That stirs her soul within the night
The softest touch of sunlit rays
She smiles within her blissful haze

The Union of the Rose and the Sun

From the depths of despair, I cried out your name
I wept and you listened in a moment you came
You spoke to me softly sweet poems of love
I knew from that moment you were sent from above
You travelled within me, you healed all my wounds
You dried off my tears, sweet solace I found
In your arms I lay still as you gave me your crown
Such warmth in your touch spun my world upside down
I curl up and feel you, I lie in your arms
For this is the place I'm protected from harm

Reaching for Sunlight

Stretching up to find you
Sometimes far beyond my grasp
My roots pull me back and I weep
The saltiness of the tears
Stinging against my skin
This earth pulls me down
I hear you calling my name
In the distance whispering
Softly words in the breeze
I am enchanted by your spell
I feel the warmth of your light
Drying off my watery tears
Soothing my stinging petals
Craving your kiss
I stretch again this time
A little closer to you
Feeling your heat warming

My every cell and burning

Me with your desire

Devotion of a Rose

I awaken to thoughts of your love in my mind
Within my Rose centre is where you I find
I open my petals and with joy receive
Your sunlight illumines my flowers and leaves
I feed on your warmth, in my garden I flower
I share my sweet fragrance with you every hour
You're the reason I open my petals each morn
My love, my devotion to you I am sworn

Divine Love

The beautiful union of a Rose and the Sun
Together in love a new dawn has begun
For once she awakens, they're never apart
She fills all her petals with love in her heart
For it is so true that love conquers all
A Rose is still love when her last petal falls
Love never ends, there is no demise
As long as the Sun shines its rays where she lies

The Solitary Rose

A Rose in her garden, a solitary bed
Quite happy alone but she raises her head
To send out her fragrance and rise to the Sun
For this is true love from where all has begun
She opens her petals on every new dawn
Releasing her scent, his rays are so warm
The pure Divine lovers, the Sun and the Rose
Entwined in their garden and so my words close

The Moonlit Rose

She lies beneath the starry skies
Awaiting dawn where her heart lies
His heat. reflections of the moon
She soaks it up, her petals swoon
She gazes up and gives a sigh
Of purest bliss beneath his sky
And settles down in deepest sleep
Within her bosom finds him deep
She curls him in her fragrant petals
The moonlit Rose in slumber settles

The Rose Bed

We lie down on our marriage bed
You softly stroke my purest head
I gaze upon your sunlit face
In bliss at home in our embrace
The stillness in your arms I crave
My beating heart for you I save
Enduring all so I can be
Forever yours, forever free

Awakening

She rises and wakes from her warm, cosy bed
Discovering light as she stretches ahead
The light of the Sun helps her blossom and grow
Her stem keeps on rising though rooted below
She stretches, receiving the Sun's warmest kiss
Enjoying a taste of eternity's bliss
For once she receives this, forever the urge
To dissolve in the Sun, so together they merge
The Rose and the Sun shining bright from above
When they find each other become purest love

Sunbathing

A Rose in her bed on a hot summer's day
Will bask in the Sun and in heaven she stays
She lifts her blossoms in thanks for the light
She sends out her fragrance with all her might
So all other flowers can feel her love flow
Knowing the kiss of true love never goes

Two become One

Open your heart and let your thoughts drift
Memories rise just allow them to sift
Stillness will come when you sit and let be
Together are we, I am you, you are me
United we live in the stillness within
One heart with a memory of how we begin
The Rose as she lies in her soft petalled bed
Soaks up the sunlight from which she is fed
She knows of its presence in her garden of light
The flowers around her unaware of her sight
The sunlight that shines on her beautiful flower
With the light of the Sun, the source of her power
Is found deep within her sweet flower that blooms
The essence and fragrance together in tune
In harmony, peace both the Sun and the Rose
Are merged with each other in beautiful prose
Both settle in Eden as two become one
They bathe in their light as the Rose and the Sun

A Pause for Devotion

With sacred Rose your feet I bathe
Each toe I kiss one by one
Anointing each with purest lips
Blessed by a Rose

I allow myself to be plucked by your love
As I withdraw my thorns for your care
I open my blooms, inhale my sweet fragrance
As I lay in your palm, I am laid bare

The song of love flows from his lips
Sets sail to sea, a thousand ships
The Rose soft petals, thorns so sharp
She raises to his purest harp
The words he sings of love so pure
She sighs upon her foreign shore

Beyond the land of setting Sun
From where this tale of love begun
There lies a man of purest heart
His love he shares, his greatest art
The softest gaze upon his face
The warmest touch in his embrace
His mind the hum of purest sound
His feet they merge in holy ground
His pure love rests upon her shore
She sings of love forever more

With sunlight you fill every petal, each bloom
I raise up my stem, all your love I consume
I swallow your essence as water I drink
My stem, it lifts higher, my roots in earth sink
I fill with your fragrance, your scent I release
To give other blossoms a taste of my peace

Softening Rays

The Rose while she's gazing high up at the Sun
She bathes in his rays, and she knows they are one
She's bringing his sunlight into the garden
To share with the flowers whose petals have hardened
The Rose is the mother, to all love she spreads
She always feels sunlight by raising her head
The light that she feels is the purest of love
Received from her lover the Sun high above
She stores in her heart, and she sends far and wide
In hope, love and peace all the flowers will find

Adoration

You fill my heart with purest fire
I burn within with such desire
I raise to meet your highest light
I feel your warmth with such delight
I'm wrapped in rays, so we are one
I bathe forever in your Sun

Two Flames

There sometimes arises upon this great earth
A ray of the Sun in two bodies is birthed
Two flames of one ray, they are Shakti and Shiva
Embodied on earth, the Devi and Deva
Their purpose in life to together unite
Bringing to earth the most powerful light
The flame that's eternal on earth in two sparks
They heal what is broken, they're one Divine heart
When they come together then two becomes three
The mother, the father and son, trinity
The Rose and the Sun, they are love, they are free
Forever entwined ever one, as are we

Rising with the Sun

The Rose she rises with the Sun
Together merged, forever one
She finds the Sun within her heart
And knows they've never been apart
In every petal, all her leaves
Her purest fragrance that she breathes
Will drop her thorns that sometimes harden
For she is the Sun, she is the garden

Rose at Dawn

The Rose at dawn she lifts her gaze
And soaks up all the morning rays
She feels its warmth upon her tips
Her words of love fall from her lips
She sees the Sun's rays never end
To all on earth its warmth it sends
It touches all and spreads for miles
Her garden filled with sunlit smiles

Unconditional Love

The Rose with her love for the Sun she adores
With growth it has deepened like never before
No conditions to give, she will love nonetheless
Expects from him nothing, she knows she is blessed
Forever she stretches her petals so all
Will feel the Sun's kiss, as they grow strong and tall
With peace she send fragrance of love all around
Her seedlings grow strong as they root in the ground
The highest of love, the love of Divine
Transforming and turning the water to wine

The Rose's Muse

The reason a Rose gives her sight to the Sun
She knows what she focuses on she becomes
The Sun is the brightest of light that there is
The source of creation, she blows it a kiss
The purest of love lifts her high like a bird
The Sun is her muse, it guides every word
She sings all her sonnets to send it her love
It fills her with joy and lifts her above
For all is vibration, the Sun lights her way
In love's purest presence is where she will stay

The Naked Rose

I lay naked in your garden
Flowers open to your scent
As you breathe in my pure fragrance
A pure love of heaven sent
You may feel my softest petals
Touch my bloom with tender care
Whisper words of sweet desire
As my petals open bare
Laying peaceful in your garden
Softest stem with no more thorns
I will rise to your desire
With devotion I am sworn

Realisation of the Rose

The Rose who understood her soul
Saw all connected as a whole
No separation from the Sun
The two in Union always one

The Rose who understood her Self
Saw all as perfect, all in health
For on her journey to the light
Her focus on true love, her sight

She realised all is deep inside
Within her petals love resides
No need to search on yonder shores
She settles in her peace once more

Allows herself to rest and heal
Just happy in the love she feels
Her love within is all she needs
On purest light within she feeds

The Quiet Rose

The Rose has times when words don't come
She sits beneath the burning Sun
The gentle touch of purest rays
Can fill her up within for days
No need to speak, just share her love
Keep focusing on high above

Smiling on the Breeze

She smiles as the breeze forms your face in the clouds
She whispers her love as she stands tall and proud
She arches her stem when receiving your kiss
Her flower it glows with your heavenly bliss
She wilts when she loses the touch of your love
So grateful when feeling your warmth from above
The reason she sings all her sonnets and prose
Her words of devotion to you from a Rose

Soaking up Rays

She lies in the Sun, and she soaks up his rays
She could lie there for hours, for weeks or for days
She opens her petals in fullness to breathe
The warmth of the sunlight, her flower receives
So blissful, so happy, her love she must share
To all in her garden, to all flowers there

Opening Petals

For a Rose to be filled with the heat of the Sun
She knows she must open each petal, each one
For nothing can fill up the heart of the Rose
If she keeps her petals inside tightly closed
For love's always flowing, she gives and receives
If she does not open, she'll harden and grieve
So keeping her flower wide open a must
To love she surrenders, the Sun she will trust

Forever Flowering

A perfect Rose forever flowers
She knows in truth there are no hours
In every moment sends her scent
To all formed of the elements
Pure love she sees in all she sends
No need to worry or pretend
The peace of knowing we are one
Within the garden of the Sun

The Sleeping Rose

The Rose in her bed she so peacefully slept
Sweet dreams of her love and the promises kept
For the Sun gave his word that forever he'd shine
In the bloom of her heart they are always entwined
So her petals stay open, they are always apart
She feels her love blooming, his warmth in her heart
She lies in bed dreaming yet ever awake
The kiss of the Sun from her slumber did shake

Soft Petals

As I lie within your garden
My soft petals shimmer and glisten
In anticipation of your rays
Filling my purest heart
With your glorious sunlight
I stretch and raise to you
My beloved one

Forever Yours

I dance in your garden
Swim naked in your ocean
Soar high above your clouds
Drift into your sunlit skies
Sit upon the tallest spires
Lay within your canopy
Allow my petals to fall
I am forever yours

Solar Power

The Rose she grew, she lifted high
Her petals opened wide
Her thorny stem left far behind
The sunlight bright inside

The Rose in union with her love
Upon her garden gazed
The Sun in all though may be dim
She hoped their light would raise

The Rose she fed upon her love
She stored within her flower
So in love's garden shared her scent
Filled all with solar power

Sacred Bed

As I lay within my garden
In my sacred bed I lie
I give my heart forever
To the Sun within the sky
One day the heavens opened
With its rays, gave me a kiss
Giving me a taste eternal
Of its radiating bliss

As I lay within my garden
Now my heart forever yours
I surrender every moment
To the one that I adore
As I settle in your sunlight
In your rays I gently bathe
Letting all just be around me
For your love my soul has saved

The One

She Rose to meet him in her dreams
The garden of the Sun
She kept her love for him alone
She knew he was the one
She grew to catch his sunny rays
Did everything she could
To reach great heights, to feel his touch
With petals stretched she stood
She pulled his sunlight down to earth
So all could feel his heat
Her fragrance strong to fill them all
From head then down to feet
The Rose, she met him in her dreams
But truly wide awake
Kept rooted on this precious earth
For all her flowers' sake

Two Souls United

In the blink of an eye, she awoke and arose
Her petals they opened, the beautiful Rose
For she had received the pure kiss of true love
He entered her world, and she soared high above
The light of his Sun soon devoured the dark
Her memories before of her lover were stark
For two souls united the Rose and the Sun
Their journey of true love had only begun

Her Perfect Garden

The Rose as she gazes high up at the Sun
She turns her awareness to all that is fun
So grateful to see all the beauty around
The scent of the flowers that lay on the ground
She loves all her petals, her stem and her leaves
Each droplet of rain and the air that she breathes
All is so perfect, for all is the Sun
She knows there is nothing but love in each one

The Heart of the Rose

The Rose she will love
Always loves without reason
Though storms they will come
Through each changing of season
She opens her petals
With stem strong and firm
Keeps raising her head
To the love that she years
For nothing she craves
But to share love with all
In her garden of flowers
To help them grow tall
And so, in this story
This song full of prose
She sends out her fragrance
The essence of Rose

The Journey's End

The Rose on her journey to greet the pure Sun
She gives it a kiss as her journey is done
She rests in her bliss and allows things to settle
So filled with its warmth within every petal
She looks at her garden so perfect and calm
She sees there are weeds but they do her no harm
For nothing can harm her for she is the Sun
Her petals and stem and her thorns are just fun

ABOUT THE AUTHORS

Vinod C V is an Assistant Professor of Sociology at Government Arts and Science College, Karungappally, Kollam, affiliated with the University of Kerala, India.

Samantha Funnell owns and runs a Vegan Skincare business with her daughter from home in Glastonbury UK.

Both have a love for poetry and philosophy.

